The King of the Lam

In Memory of Liam Ó Muirthile

Greg Delanty

First published in 2020
by Southword Editions
The Munster Literature Centre
Frank O'Connor House, 84 Douglas Street
Cork, Ireland

Set in Adobe Caslon 12pt

THE KING OF THE LAM

Contents

The Shaky Bridge

An droichead crochta
a bhainimis amach
chun é a chroitheadh
le spleodar óige amháin.

Samhail gan meirg gan mairg
idir bruacha dhá theanga
ag croitheadh i mbun dáin:
Droichead Uí Ríordáin.

Liam Ó Muirthile

Caoineadh

Nothing matches this man's going. I have filled leaves
of a thick notebook. Something savage, a deep moan
is called for, befitting an ancient keen, the grieves
breaking through the vortex of ink. A heavy stone
can't be budged. I am left with one word: *leaves*
and the un-word of a *gol*, the act of an Irish *ochón*.

Our Paradise

Liam lies in the cemetery of Saint Gobnait.
Passing by bus, I stand, wave to him. Other passengers
    are naturally unsettled — I'm beyond caring
      why puzzled strangers
      shift seats. They'd understand had they met
him. They'd bow instead of staring

at the loony, pray with me to the bees — Gobnait's
emissaries on their June ministry —
    to beseech the order of maggots, selflessly
      devoting themselves to his body,
    cowled in their order's white habits,
assisted by selfless sects of worms — to be

especially kind to this man; to deliver
him unto the trees he loved: ash, Irish yew,
    silver birch, elm, oak; to the common and rare;
      resurrect him, allow him accrue
    and renew the peculiar character,
the *blas* issuing from the earth and air

of this, his resting place. May perpetual light
shine on him, for he more than any was our haven:
    our air, fire, water, earth. I'm trying to be concise.
      Carry him in a slow procession
    with humble ceremony out of declining sight.
Sound the pipes, a corker man enters our paradise.

Tombstone

How we love a laugh. Excuse me, past tense.
Loved. We were always pulling the leg
of any day. You and I never had much sense,
nor wanted any. You weren't Liam, nor I Greg,
but Billy the Kid and Stoney Burke, whatever peg

we could hang a laugh off of, riding the bronco
of staying up. When all is laughed and done
humour's the safety catch released, our live ammo.
My Winchester's out of caps and my cork gun
has lost its cork, the string snapped, the silver one

I picked out, as you did, in McCarthy's toyshop
on Douglas Street. What'll I do, Billy,
without you. Confound it. I can't even hop
on the blower. There's no possibility
of getting through to you. No one to help me

back on the high donkey of poetry. Liam, Kid, Bill,
remember riding into Tombstone, nine-shooters ready,
covering one another's back. Now who will
pick off the gringo, gunslinger, villain, vigilante
on the saloon roof? Just a matter of time, Delanty.

After a Death

I tell myself how lucky I am to have had such a friend,
that I must be grateful, must watch my attitude,
keep it together. He'll remain with me till my own end.
But that luck's turned unlucky, shrouding gratitude.

The Lam Partners

I don't know anyone who loved going on the lam
   more than you. Mobiles off and us gone for days
on a drive-about, tired of giving a damn
   about the world, taking all the byways

we could; you striking up talk with this or that stranger
   as if you'd known them all your life.
You switched off their modern cagey and danger
   buttons — I could practically see regular strife

fall from them outside a petrol pump station,
   pharmacy or grocery store. How often did I
witness this knack of yours with silent admiration,
   you leaving them laughing and us off on the fly.

Nor did I say how I thrived in your company,
   felt sound myself, us off to wherever:
Bolus, Spanish Point, Roaring Water, Ballyvourney
   with Margaret Barry, Cooley, Dylan (whoever

fitted the mood and theme of whatever high or low)
   accompanying every turn the spur
of our moments took us: up, down, across, below
   in the Nirvana, Shangri-la, Valhalla, Big Sur

of us being on the road. Only weeks have past
   since we schemed, planned another big trip,
frontiersmen about to head into the wild west,
   cut a blazing trail into the time-honoured map

of poetry, landscape, *dinnshenchas.* You should know
   that your last drive was taken instead
on your own in the back of a flashy black limo,
   tailed west across Ireland. The king of the lam is dead.

I only copped after trailing you that day which letter
   is left when you take the lam away from Liam —
my dead-end word game diverting this lone character —
   and that *lam* is only nearly a full-rhyme with your name.

At Sea

An astronaut's mooring to the mother ship
snaps and he falls away into the ink –
black universe;

an unconscious lone survivor
is adrift
in a lifeboat;

a bell diver
deep in a wreck tugs thrice — all
he's left with is a chewed-up cord.

Old flicks we clung to in the Savoy Cinema,
so transported that we couldn't fathom who ate
our popcorn, ice lolls, those extinct macaroon bars.

*

You swore as good as any Cork man worth his salt,
said that you were living, breathing
and drowning in a dying language,

and I, trying to keep you afloat, replying
"Come on, Liamo, if that's so, then what
a great muse opportunity. Use it, man";

the Irish language itself being cut loose,
dragged under by the drowning-embrace
of oblivion, the only certain eternity;

how all life goes belly-up eventually,
as will the queen's English even,
(did I catch a bitteen of a smile at that?):

Shelley, Keats and Shakespeare. Gone
as if they never were. It didn't sink in
till you were being lowered into the grave haltingly

like a lifeboat from the side of a ship (save it was
the varnished death boat of your gilt-handled box)
that you now pilot the only unifying tradition.

Ligature

I'll give Liam an ol' bell. Wake up: Liam is history.
The line between long and short-term memory

is out of whack. I just wanted to make a quick call,
ask how things are. Meet me behind the walnut oil,

the soot, turpentine, the dye, this concoction of ink.
We are most at home here. What do you think

of this latest one? Should I drop the first line?
Afterwords we'll take a scove if the weather's fine,

shanksmare over Patrick's Bridge, take our ease,
chat with whoever. No better than you to shoot *da* breeze.

We'll call up to my dad in Eagle Printing. Talk shop,
the dumping of word worlds; hellboxing the latest job:

live and dead matter, the breaking of gadzook,
of the ligature connecting all our lives. Liam look,

its near clock-out time. Ye two would've such rapport.
We'll catch him coming out the Phoenix Street door.

Munster

We never finished our on-hold confabulation:
the uncharted South, how we were by nature
word-lizarding, palm-tree spouting, wild fuchsia-
blazing, warmed more with a Mediterranean

and gulf-stream temperament. Márquez, Lorca,
ye're just trotting after us. As much Neruda
as Jorge Luis Borges. We've nothing to gain
except our selves, our own magic reality, apart

but still a part of the double-verse of our island.
We are the more colourful ones, Latino by heart.
I'm leading our Pegasus, our choleric Rocinante
to the front of the Irish cart, standing our ground.

But you are fresh in the Cork earth and I, Delanty,
am the lone hidalgo, babbling away, far from sound.

Phantom Talk

Time cures all. "Jesus wept." A poet in the prime
of his gift the newspaper said. Time's a shagging thief.
"Wow, that's new." I hear you. If time pilfers grief, this rhyme
admits it will steal you from us. You give me grief

from the otherworld of my sense that you're still with us,
a phantom friend, which, barring your poems, is all
we have. A big all, for sure. Regards to folks on Parnassus.
Find a place to attach this on your side of the wall

(the one we can climb over only once, no more)
the way a hand sticks a photo of a child or friend,
a wise quote or list of to-do on the fridge door.
Yes, I know this notice is pointless in the end,

a missing person's mugshot flapping on a wall, a torn sign,
the search long called off. The mug is not yours, but mine.

Envoy

The Shaky Bridge

The suspension bridge
we sought it out
only to give it a good shake
with the gusto of youth.

Symbol without rust without regret
between the banks of two languages
shaking with the frenzy of poetry:
Ó Ríordáin Bridge.

Acknowledgements

The Irish Times: Tombstone
Southword: Our Paradise

Liam Ó Muirthile poem "The Shaky Bridge" is the epigraph poem. ©
Liam Ó Muirthile. From *An Fuíoll Feá – Rogha Dánta*. Cois Life 2013.

"The Shaky Bridge" is translated by Greg Delanty as the envoy poem.

I would like to thank Jonathan Williams for his help and those friends
who helped with earlier drafts of the poems.